A Gift for

Date

From

JOHN MACARTHUR

The Extraordinary
MOTHER

Blessings for You from Bible Moms

Published by
THOMAS NELSON™
Since 1798

www.thomasnelson.com

Table of Contents

No matter what her other virtues—a generous nature, a gift for hospitality, beauty, intelligence, culinary expertise, an excellent wife to her husband or mother to her children, a community leader—nothing makes a woman more extraordinary than her faith. This was true in Bible times, and it still applies today.

The Extraordinary Mother demonstrates this big truth by exploring the ways that many women in the Bible still offer extraordinary lessons for mothers today. Not every woman in this book is an unwavering example of godly virtue. In fact, most of them have significant flaws. But they all are distinguished by their faith (or, in a few cases, by their lack of it).

Faith makes a woman

Most of these women are mothers by birth. A few are mothers by behavior. We know many of them waited long years for God to grant them children. Some raised children of great faith; others were disappointed. Some great mothers are even unnamed. But all of them can teach us something valuable about what makes a woman—particularly a mother—truly extraordinary.

As you read the stories of these mothers and consider the blessings available from their examples, may you grow in your own faith and in how you're able to nurture the Spirit of God in your own family and community.

extraordinary.

Eve

THE MOTHER OF ALL THE LIVING

Genesis 1–3

*E*ve must have been a creature of unsurpassed beauty. She was the crown and the pinnacle of God's amazing creative work, the last living thing to be called into existence—actually fashioned directly by the Creator's own hand in a way that showed particular care and attention to detail. Adam was refined dirt; Eve was a glorious refinement of humanity itself. She was Adam's necessary partner who finally made his existence complete— and whose own existence finally signaled the completion of all creation.

If the man represented the supreme species (a race of creatures made in the image of God), Eve was the living embodiment of humanity's glory (1 Corinthians 11:7). God had truly saved the best for last.

Eve was the flawless archetype of feminine excellence. Because no other woman has ever come into a curse-free world, no other woman could possibly surpass Eve's grace, charm, virtue, ingenuity, intelligence, wit, and pure innocence. Physically, too, she must have personified all the best traits of both strength and beauty. Scripture gives us no physical description of Eve. Her beauty—splendid as it must have been—is never mentioned or even alluded to. The focus of the biblical account is on Eve's relationships with her Creator and her husband.

As "the mother of all living" (Genesis 3:20), Eve is a major character in the story of humanity's fall and redemption. Yet in all of Scripture, her name is used only four times—twice in the Old Testament (Genesis 3:20; 4:1), and twice in the New Testament (2 Corinthians 11:3; 1 Timothy 2:13). Not only is no physical description of her given; we don't even know such details as how many children she had, how long she lived, or where and how she died (Genesis 5:3–5).

Eve's creation reminds us of several crucial truths about womanhood in general. It speaks of Eve's fundamental equality with Adam. The woman was "taken out of man" (Genesis 2:23). She was of exactly the same essence as Adam. She was in no way an inferior character, but she was his spiritual
counterpart, his intellectual coequal, and in every sense his perfect mate and companion. Her creation also reminds us of the essential unity that is the ideal in every marriage relationship, and it illustrates how deep and meaningful the marriage of husband and wife is designed to be. It is not merely a physical union, but a union of heart and soul as well. The intimacy of her relationship with her husband is rooted in the fact that she was literally taken from his side.

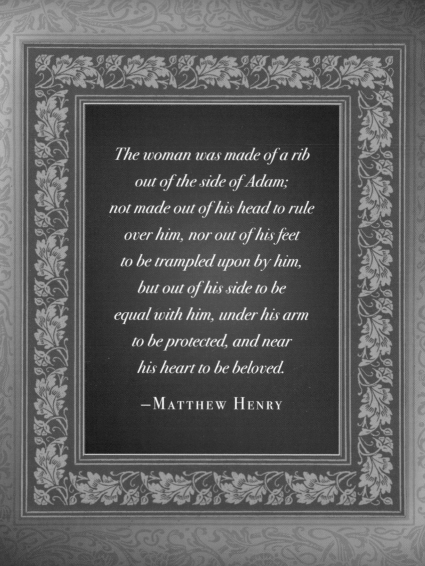

The woman was made of a rib
out of the side of Adam;
not made out of his head to rule
over him, nor out of his feet
to be trampled upon by him,
but out of his side to be
equal with him, under his arm
to be protected, and near
his heart to be beloved.

—MATTHEW HENRY

Eve's creation also contains some important biblical lessons about the divinely designed role of women. Although Eve was spiritually and intellectually Adam's peer; although they were both of one essence and therefore equals in their standing before God and in their rank above the other creatures; there was nonetheless a clear distinction in their earthly roles. Adam was designed to be a father, provider, protector, and leader. Eve was designed to be a mother, comforter, nurturer, and helper. To acknowledge that there are such fundamental differences between the genders may not correspond with modern feminist sensibilities, but this is what God's own Word says.

After creation and before the fall, Adam and Eve were partners and companions, fellow-laborers in the garden. God dealt with Adam as head of the human race, and Eve was accountable to her husband. This was true paradise, and they constituted a perfect microcosm of the human race as God designed it to be.

But then it was all ruined by sin. The chronology of the account seems to suggest that a very short time elapsed between the end of Creation (Genesis 1:31) and the fall of Satan (Isaiah 14:12–15;

Ezekiel 28:12–19). A similarly short time appears to have elapsed between Satan's fall and Eve's temptation. It might have been only a few days—or perhaps even only a matter of hours. But it could not have been very long. Adam and Eve had not yet even conceived any children. The tempter wasted no time deceiving Eve and provoking her husband to sin. He wanted to strike before the race had any opportunity to multiply. If he could beguile Eve and thereby cause Adam to fall at this moment, he could sabotage all of humanity in one deadly act of treason against God.

Satan singled out Eve for his cunning deception when she was not in the company of Adam. Away from her husband, but close to the forbidden tree, she was in the most vulnerable position possible. It is likely that Eve had heard about God's only restriction not directly from God but from her husband. Genesis 2:16–17 records that God gave the prohibition just prior to her creation, at a time when Adam must have been the lone recipient. Eve's instruction and her protection were Adam's responsibility, but Satan found her alone and apparently without accurate understanding of God's warning to Adam.

Eve was deceived. She "saw that the tree was good for food, that it was pleasant to the eyes, and a tree desirable to make one wise" (Genesis 3:6). Notice the natural desires that contributed to Eve's confusion: her bodily appetites (it was good for food); her aesthetic sensibilities (it was pleasant to the eyes); and her intellectual curiosity (it was desirable for wisdom). Those are all good, legitimate, healthy urges—unless the object of desire is sinful, and then natural passion becomes evil lust. That can never result in any good. Eve ate, and then she gave to her husband to eat.

Even though Eve was deceived into eating the forbidden fruit—rather than acting out of deliberate disobedience—her sin still subjected her to God's displeasure. She forfeited the paradise of Eden and inherited a life of pain and frustration instead. No matter what means Satan may use to beguile us into sin—no matter how subtle his cunning—the responsibility for the deed itself still lies with the sinner and no one else. Eve could not escape accountability for what she had done by transferring the blame (Genesis 3:13).

That accountability resulted in serious ramifications that women struggle with even to this day. God place a curse on Eve (vs. 16) that deals with the two most important relationships in which a woman might naturally seek her highest joy: her husband and her children. "To the woman He said: 'I will greatly multiply your sorrow and your conception; In pain you shall bring forth children; Your desire shall be for your husband, And he shall rule over you.'" In a fallen world, sadness, pain, and physical difficulties would be part and parcel of the woman's daily routine. In childbirth, however, the pain and sorrow would be "greatly multiplied." The bearing of children, which originally had the potential to bring the most undiluted kind of joy and gladness, would instead be marred by severe pain and difficulty. The second part of the verse is a little harder to interpret: "Your desire shall be for your husband, and he shall rule over you."

Before Adam sinned, his leadership was always perfectly wise and loving and tender. Before Eve sinned, her submission was the perfect model of meekness and modesty. But sin changed all of that. She would now chafe under his headship and desire to gain dominance over him. His tendency would be to suppress her in a harsh or domineering way. And thus we see that tensions over gender roles go all the way back to our first parents.

The severity of the curse must have shattered Eve's heart, but God's judgment was not entirely harsh and hopeless. There was a good deal of grace, even in the curse. To the eyes of faith, there were rays of hope that shone even through the cloud of God's displeasure. Although their relationship would now have tensions that did not exist in Eden, Eve remained Adam's partner. She retained her role as a wife, and she would still be the mother of all living (v. 20).

The promise that Eve would still bear children mitigated every other aspect of the curse. That one simple expectation contained a ray of hope for the whole human race. There was a hint in the curse itself that one of Eve's own offspring would ultimately overthrow evil and dispel all the darkness of sin. Eve had set a whole world of evil in motion by her disobedience; now, through her offspring, she would produce a Savior. This powerful hope had already been implicitly given to her, in the portion of the curse where the Lord addressed the evil spirit indwelling the snake: "I will put enmity . . . between your seed and her Seed; He shall bruise your head, and you shall bruise His heel" (v. 15). Eve must have taken heart from this guarantee that her race would not be hopelessly subordinated to the evil one's domination forever. The curse against the serpent held a promise for Eve: her own offspring would destroy the destroyer.

Christ, who was uniquely "born of a woman" (Galatians 4:4)—the offspring of a virgin, and God in human form—literally fulfilled this promise that the Seed of the woman would break the serpent's head.

It is clear that Eve's hope was personified in her own children. She saw them as tokens of God's goodness and reminders of the promise that her Seed would be the instrument by which the tempter's ultimate destruction was accomplished. For instance, in her great joy upon first becoming a mother, Eve said, "I have acquired a man from the LORD"

(Genesis 4:1). It was an expression of hope and rejoicing because of God's grace, compassion, kindness, and forgiveness toward her. When Eve bore Seth—after Cain had already broken her heart by murdering Abel—Scripture says, she "named him Seth [meaning, "appointed one"], 'For God has appointed another seed for me instead of Abel, whom Cain killed'" (v. 25). The reference to the "appointed seed" suggests that her heart had laid hold of the promise concealed in the curse, and she treasured the undying hope that one day her own Seed would fulfill that promise.

A Blessing for You

May you imbue your children
with love of their Creator, joy in His unique roles
for them, and faith that He will guide them safely
into the blessed life beyond the curse.

Sarah

A PICTURE OF FAITH IN GOD'S PROMISES

Genesis 11–21

From the day Sarah became the wife of the great patriarch Abraham, she desired one thing above all else: to have children. But she was barren throughout her normal childbearing years. That is practically the first thing Scripture mentions about Sarah. After recording her marriage to Abraham (Genesis 11:29), the next verse says, *"But Sarai was barren; she had no child."* That one statement sums up everything Scripture has to say about the first sixty-five years of her life.

Sarah was obviously tortured by her childlessness. Every recorded episode of ill temper or strife in her household was related to her frustrations about her own barrenness. It ate at her. She spent years gripped by frustration and depression because of it. She desperately wanted to be a mother, but she finally concluded that God Himself was restraining her from having children (Genesis 16:2).

A study in contrasts and contradictions, Sarah was indeed one extraordinary woman. Her faith sometimes vacillated, but that faith persevered against unbelievable obstacles and became one of the central features of her legacy. In fact, the New Testament enshrines her in the Hall of Faith: "*because she judged Him faithful who had promised*" (Hebrews 11:11). Although she had terrible flashes of petulance and even cruelty, Sarah's life on the whole is characterized by humility, meekness, hospitality, faithfulness, deep affection for her husband, sincere love toward God, and hope that never died.

The full spectacle of Sarah's amazing faith doesn't really become apparent until we contemplate the many seemingly insurmountable obstacles to that faith.

Abraham and Sarah both came from an urban environment. They did not start wandering until Abraham was already in his mid-seventies and Sarah was only a decade behind that. Life on the road was not something Sarah was accustomed to; it was something she had to learn to embrace.

What energized Sarah's willingness to leave all familiar surroundings, sever ties with her family, and commit to a life of rootless wandering?

She knew of the vast promise God had made to Abraham: "*I will make you a great nation; I will bless you and make your name great; and you shall be a blessing. I will bless those who bless you, and I will curse him who curses you; and in you all the families of the earth shall be blessed*" (Genesis 12:2–3). God's promise was unconditional and literally unlimited in the scope of its blessings. God would bless Abraham, make him a blessing, and make him a vehicle through which blessing would come to the whole world. The promised blessing even had eternal implications. Sarah understood that promise. According to

Scripture, she believed it (Hebrews 11:11). Sarah obviously had a key role to play in this plan. Abraham could never become the patriarch of a great nation if she did not first become mother to his children.

Despite her faith, however, she knew from a human perspective that her long years of childlessness already loomed large as a threat to the fulfillment of God's pledge. Sarah must have constantly pondered these things, and as time went by, the weight of her burden only increased.

We can understand Sarah's despair. Ten more fruitless years passed after Abraham and Sarah arrived in Canaan (Genesis 16:3). Sarah was now seventy-five years old, post-menopausal, and still childless. If God planned to make her the mother of Abraham's heir, why had He not done so by now? It was natural for her to think God was deliberately withholding children from her. As a matter of fact, He was. When His time came for the promise to be fulfilled, no one would be able to deny that this was indeed God's doing. His plan all along was for Sarah to have her first child in her old age, after every prospect of a natural fulfillment of the prophecy was exhausted and after every earthly reason for hope was dead. Thus YHWH would put His power on display.

But as she considered her circumstances, Sarah concluded that a kind of surrogate parenting was the only possible solution to her predicament. If God's promise to Abraham was ever going to be fulfilled, Abraham had to father children by some means. Sarah thus unwittingly took it upon herself to try to engineer a fulfillment of the divine promise to Abraham. She stepped into the role of God.

Sarah had a maidservant, named Hagar, whom she had acquired during their time in Egypt. Sarah apparently reasoned that because she owned Hagar, if Abraham fathered a child by Hagar, it would in effect be Sarah's child. "*So Sarai said to Abram, 'See now, the LORD has restrained me from bearing children. Please, go in to my maid; perhaps I shall obtain children by her.' And Abram heeded the voice of Sarai*" (Genesis 16:2).

Sarah's faith resided in promises God had made to Abraham. Up to this point, Sarah had never explicitly been named in the covenant God made with Abraham. That was her hope and expectation. But the episode with Hagar shows that Sarah's hope was beginning to wane. She was slowly losing heart. When Ishmael was born to Hagar, Scripture says Abraham was eighty-six years old (v. 16). Thirteen more frustrating, barren years passed for Sarah after that. If her hope was not already shattered, it must have hung by a very thin thread.

Finally, when Abraham was ninety-nine, the Lord appeared to him again, and for the first time on record, He specifically brought Sarah by name into the covenant promises: "*Then God said to Abraham, 'As for Sarai your wife, you shall not call her name Sarai ["my princess"], but Sarah ["Princess"] shall be her name. And I will bless her and also give you a son by her; then I will bless her, and she shall be a mother of nations; kings of peoples shall be from her. . . . Sarah your wife shall bear you a son, and you shall call his name Isaac. . . . My covenant I will establish with Isaac, whom Sarah shall bear to you at this set time next year'*" (17:15–16, 19, 21). For the first time, here was a clear promise, with a fixed date, assuring Sarah of her place in the covenant.

The year that followed was a difficult and busy year for Abraham and Sarah. That was the year God destroyed Sodom and Gomorrah (18:16 – 19:29). And during that same year, Abraham journeyed south into the land ruled by Abimelech, king of Gerar. Sarah, though now ninety, was still beautiful enough to stir the passions of a king. What had happened in Egypt twenty-five years earlier was replayed once more. Abraham tried to pass Sarah off as his sister, and Abimelech, smitten with her beauty, began to pursue her. But God warned Abimelech in a dream that she was Abraham's wife (20:3), so he did not touch her (v. 6).

Immediately after that incident, "*The LORD visited Sarah as He had said, and the LORD did for Sarah as He had spoken. For Sarah conceived and bore Abraham a son in his old age, at the set time of which God had spoken to him*" (21:1–2). Sarah named him Isaac, meaning "laughter." And Sarah said, "*God has made me laugh, and all who hear will laugh with me*" (v. 6). We're given a fascinating insight into Sarah's character by the fact that she saw genuine humor in the way God had dealt with her. "*Who would have said to Abraham that Sarah would nurse children? For I have borne him a son in his old age*" (v. 7).

Despite her occasional bursts of temper and struggles with discouragement, Sarah remained an essentially good-humored woman. After those long years of bitter frustration, she could still appreciate the irony and relish the comedy of becoming a mother at such an old age. Her life's ambition was now realized, and the memory of years of bitter disappointment quickly disappeared from view. God had indeed been faithful.

Sarah plays a major role in only one more episode recounted by Scripture. Isaac was finally weaned—and from what we know of the culture, he would therefore have been a young toddler, probably two or three years old. It was a time for celebration. But something happened that was the final straw for Sarah in her long struggle to accept Hagar as her husband's concubine. She saw Ishmael making fun of Isaac (v. 9). She immediately said, *"Cast out this bondwoman and her son; for the son of this bondwoman shall not be heir with my son, namely with Isaac"* (v. 10).

Virtually any woman forced to share her husband with a concubine would respond to a situation like this as Sarah did.

She was Abraham's true wife. Hagar was an interloper. Besides, according to the promise of God, Isaac was Abraham's true heir, promised by God to be the one through whom the covenant blessing would eventually see fulfillment. What may appear at first glance to be an overreaction was actually another proof of Sarah's great faith in God's promise. God Himself affirmed the wisdom of her demand: "*God said to Abraham, 'Do not let it be displeasing in your sight because of the lad or because of your bondwoman. Whatever Sarah has said to you, listen to her voice; for in Isaac your seed shall be called*'" (v. 12).

The apostle Paul uses the expulsion of Hagar as an illustration of the conflict between law and grace. Hagar, the bondwoman, represents the slavery of legalism (the bondage of trying to earn favor with God through works). Sarah, the faithful wife, represents the perfect liberty of grace. Paul was reminding the Galatian believers that "*we, brethren, as Isaac was, are children of promise*"—saved by grace, not vainly hoping to be saved by works (Galatians 4:28). "*But, as he who was born according to the flesh then persecuted him who was born according to the Spirit, even so it is now*" (v. 29). The kind of religion dependent on human effort (symbolized by the carnal scheme that conceived Ishmael as an artificial fulfillment of God's promise) is utterly incompatible with divine grace (symbolized by Isaac, the heir of God's promise), and the two types of faith are so hostile to one another that they cannot even abide in close proximity.

After Hagar was cast out, Sarah returned to a healthy, monogamous life with her beloved husband and their child, Isaac, who was a perpetual reminder to both Sarah and Abraham of God's staunch faithfulness. As far as we know, the rest of her years were lived out in joy and peace.

Sarah's faith had been well tested. She clearly demonstrated her absolute trust in God's promises. And the stamp of God's approval on her is contained in those New Testament passages that recognize her for her steadfast faithfulness. In fact, in the very same way the New Testament portrays Abraham as the spiritual father of all who believe (Romans 4:9–11; Galatians 3:7), Sarah is pictured as the spiritual matriarch of all faithful women (1 Peter 3:6). Far from isolating those memorable instances where Sarah behaved badly, Scripture honors her as the epitome of a woman adorned with "*the incorruptible beauty of a gentle and quiet spirit*" (1 Peter 3:4).

A Blessing for You

May you never give up on God's promises to
you and to your family. May your children grow
up in full assurance of their place in your heart,
in your home, and in their potential as
faithful stewards of God's will.

Hagar

AN EXTRAORDINARY OPPORTUNITY LOST

Genesis 16–17

*L*et's take a moment to consider "the other woman," Hagar, an Egyptian. After many childless years, Sarah resorted to the custom of the day by which a barren wife could get a child through one of her own maidservants (Genesis 16:2). Abraham disregarded God's response to his earlier attempt to appoint an heir (15:2–5) and sinfully yielded to Sarah's insistence. After conceiving Ishmael, Hagar regarded Sarah with contempt, and consequently, Sarah treated her so badly that Hagar ran away. During this time on the run Hagar was given an extraordinary gift—a message from the Angel of the Lord, who is often identified as the pre-incarnate Christ. Hagar recognized that in seeing this Angel, she had seen God (16:13). Others who had similar experiences came to the same conclusion (Genesis 22:11–18; 31:11–13; Exodus 3:2–5; Numbers 22:22–35; Judges 6:11–23; 13:2–5; 1 Kings 19:5–7).

Now the Angel of the LORD found her by a spring of water in the wilderness, by the spring on the way to Shur. And He said, "Hagar, Sarai's maid, where have you come from, and where are you going?"

She said, "I am fleeing from the presence of my mistress Sarai."

The Angel of the LORD said to her, "Return to your mistress, and submit yourself under her hand." Then the Angel of the LORD said to her, "I will multiply your descendants exceedingly, so that they shall not be counted for multitude." And the Angel of the LORD said to her:

"Behold, you are with child,
And you shall bear a son.

You shall call his name Ishmael,
Because the LORD has heard your affliction.
He shall be a wild man;
His hand shall be against every man,
And every man's hand against him.
And he shall dwell in the presence of all his brethren."

Then she called the name of the LORD who spoke to her,
You–Are–the–God–Who–Sees; for she said, "Have I also here
seen Him who sees me?" Therefore the well was called Beer
Lahai Roi; observe, it is between Kadesh and Bered.

So Hagar bore Abram a son; and Abram named his son,
whom Hagar bore, Ishmael. Abram was eighty-six years old
when Hagar bore Ishmael to Abram.

—Genesis 16:7–16

In this encounter, the Angel made it clear to Hagar that rebelling against Sarah was not the solution to her troubles (v. 9). Instead, she was to return to Abraham's encampment and trust that God would take care of her. The Angel promised Hagar that she would be the mother of innumerable descendants, people whom we know today as the Arabs. Recognizing the Angel as God, Hagar ascribed a new name to Him— *You–Are–the–God–Who–Sees*. She was astonished at having been the object of God's gracious attention. The theophany and revelation also led her to call Him *The One Who Lives and Sees Me* (v. 14).

Hagar obeyed God by returning to Sarah and Abraham, and Abraham gave their son Ishmael every opportunity to live in God's blessing. Abraham even "*said to God, 'Oh, that Ishmael might live before You!'*" To which God replied, "*As for Ishmael, I have heard you. Behold, I have blessed him, and will make him fruitful, and will multiply him exceedingly. He shall beget twelve princes, and I will make him a great nation. But My covenant I will establish with Isaac, whom Sarah shall bear to you at this set time next year.' Then He finished talking with him, and God went up from Abraham*" (Genesis 17:18, 20–22).

A woman, when she is in labor,
has sorrow because her hour has come,
but as soon as she has given birth
to the child, she no longer remembers
the anguish, for joy that a human
being has been born into the world.

—JOHN 16:21

Sure enough, Isaac was born the next year and Ishmael lost his hope of being Abraham's heir.

When Ishmael was about seventeen years old, Sarah cast him and his mother into the wilderness. As their water was used up and it seemed certain they would die, Hagar again received a miraculous visitation:

> "*The angel of God called to Hagar out of heaven, and said to her, 'What ails you, Hagar? Fear not, for God has heard the voice of the lad where he is. Arise, lift up the lad and hold him with your hand, for I will make him a great nation.' Then God opened her eyes, and she saw a well of water. And she went and filled the skin with water, and gave the lad a drink. So God was with the lad; and he grew and dwelt in the wilderness, and became an archer. He dwelt in the Wilderness of Paran; and his mother took a wife for him from the land of Egypt*" (Genesis 21:17–21).

Ishmael was raised as part of a godly household, but he failed to establish a godly legacy in his own line. Despite her two encounters with heavenly visitors, nothing in Scripture suggests that Hagar nurtured her son's faith in God. The fact that Hagar found an Egyptian wife for Ishmael suggests that she herself rejected the Lord who had sustained her and promised great blessings for her son. Perhaps she thought that if God would bless Isaac more than Ishmael, then Ishmael had no reason to put God first. The consequence is that millions of descendents of Isaac and Ishmael still despise each other today, four thousand years after their mothers parted in anger.

Hagar's example offers this warning to mothers: Your faith—or lack of it—will affect many generations to come. Don't let your anger with people of God keep you from raising children of God.

A Blessing for You

 Like Hagar, may you be blessed with extraordinary encounters with God. Unlike Hagar, may you be a mother who chooses faith no matter what adversities arise, and may your children inherit this godly legacy.

Rebekah

Her Love Knew No Bounds

Genesis 24–27

*I*saac was the miraculous son of an extraordinary promise, and after Sarah died Abraham was determined to find Isaac a worthy wife. In those days, matrimonial arrangements were made by parents, and chosen partners typically came from one's own tribe. At his age (Genesis 24:1), Abraham was concerned to perpetuate his people and God's promise through the next generation, so he covenanted with his servant to return to Mesopotamia and bring back a wife for Isaac. It was apparently customary to marry one's first cousin. But Abraham's higher motive in finding Isaac's wife among relatives four hundred fifty miles away was to prevent Isaac from marrying a Canaanite pagan, thus possibly leading the people away from the true God.

Abraham and Sarah had not lost all ties with their original home. Abraham's brother, Nahor, still lived back in Mesopotamia, though he had not seen him for about sixty years. Despite geographical separation, news about family genealogies flowed back and forth in the Fertile Crescent region, and Abraham knew of a daughter, Rebekah, born to Isaac's cousin, Bethuel (22:23). So Abraham sent his most trusted servant on the long journey to bring back a godly wife for Isaac. Arriving in the appointed town, he prayed God would show him the right woman by granting him a specific sign: the chosen bride would offer to draw water for his thirsty camels. Hospitality in those days required giving water to a thirsty stranger, but not to animals. A woman who would do that was unusually kind and served beyond the call of duty. Moreover, a single camel can hold up to twenty-five gallons, and Abraham's steward had ten of them. Serving them was a great task, but Rebekah filled them all (24:22), revealing her servant attitude (vv. 15–20) along with her beauty and purity (v. 16).

Learning who she was, "*the man bowed down his head and worshiped the LORD. And he said, 'Blessed be the LORD God of my master*

Abraham, who has not forsaken His mercy and His truth toward my master. As for me, being on the way, the LORD led me to the house of my master's brethren.' So the young woman ran and told her mother's household these things" (24:26–28).

That evening, Rebekah became betrothed to Isaac, a cousin she'd never met, and the next day she left her home and family forever. Commendably, Rebekah concurred with the servant's desire for immediate departure, and she showed her confident acceptance of what was providentially coming about in her life. In their final moments together, her family prayed that Rebekah would be blessed with numerous offspring. Little did they realize that their conventional wish fitted in nicely with God's promises of many descendants to Abraham through Sarah and Isaac. They also prayed for her offspring to be victorious over their enemies, perhaps echoing God's promises of possession of the land of the Canaanites (Genesis 13:17; 15:7, 16; 17:8).

So they sent away Rebekah their sister
and her nurse, and Abraham's servant
and his men. And they blessed
Rebekah and said to her:

"Our sister, may you become
The mother of thousands of ten thousands;
And may your descendants possess
The gates of those who hate them."

Then Rebekah and her maids arose,
and they rode on the camels and
followed the man. So the servant
took Rebekah and departed.

—Genesis 24:59–61

When Rebekah saw Isaac walking across a field to meet them, she modestly "*took a veil and covered herself*" (24:65), because convention demanded that a bride veil her face in the presence of her betrothed until the wedding day. "*And the servant told Isaac all the things that he had done. Then Isaac brought her into his mother Sarah's tent; and he took Rebekah and she became his wife, and he loved her. So Isaac was comforted after his mother's death*" (vv. 66–67). Because she wore a veil, Isaac, who was forty years old, did not see Rebekah's beauty until after he accepted her as his wife. When he did see her, "he loved her."

After their auspicious beginning, the couple faced the same problem that had plagued Sarah. Confronted by twenty years of Rebekah's barrenness (25:19, 26), Isaac rose to the test and earnestly turned to God in prayer, obviously acknowledging thereby God's involvement and timing in the seed–promise. "*The LORD granted his plea, and Rebekah his wife conceived*" (v. 21). But it was a difficult pregnancy, and Rebekah was moved to follow her husband's example and pray.

"So she went to inquire of the LORD.

And the LORD said to her:
'Two nations are in your womb,
Two peoples shall be separated from your body;
One people shall be stronger than the other,
And the older shall serve the younger.'

"So when her days were fulfilled for her to give birth, indeed there were twins in her womb. And the first came out red. He was like a hairy garment all over; so they called his name Esau. Afterward his brother came out, and his hand took hold of Esau's heel; so his name was called Jacob. Isaac was sixty years old when she bore them.

"So the boys grew. And Esau was a skillful hunter, a man of the field; but Jacob was a mild man, dwelling in tents. And Isaac loved Esau because he ate of his game, but Rebekah loved Jacob" (vv. 22–28).

Rebekah had learned directly from the Lord that the severe jostling in her womb prefigured the future antagonism between the two nations to arise from her twin sons (v. 23). She also had received divine confirmation that her younger son would be greater than her firstborn. This was contrary to the custom in patriarchal times when the elder son enjoyed the privileges of precedence in the household and at the father's death received a double share of the inheritance and became the recognized head of the family (Exodus 22:29; Numbers 8:14–17; Deuteronomy 21:17). Grave offenses could annul such primogeniture rights (Genesis 35:22; 49:3–4; 1 Chronicles 5:1) or the birthright could be sacrificed or legally transferred to another relative (Genesis 25:29–34). In this case, God declared the deviation from tradition, because His sovereign elective purposes do not necessarily have to follow custom (Romans 9:10–14).

Even though they were twins, Jacob and Esau were clearly different. The difference between the two sons manifested itself in several areas:

1. As progenitors—Esau of Edom and Jacob of Israel
2. In disposition—Esau a rugged, headstrong hunter preferring the outdoors and Jacob a plain, amiable man preferring the comforts of home
3. In parental favoritism—Esau by his father and Jacob by his mother

These were ingredients for conflict and heartache!

The struggle between the brothers came to a head when Isaac, old and blind, declared his readiness to bless Esau. Ignoring the words of God to Rebekah (Genesis 25:23), forgetting Esau's bartered birthright (v. 33), and overlooking Esau's grievous marriages (26:35), Isaac was still intent on treating Esau as the eldest and granting him the blessing of birthright, and so arranged for his favorite meal before bestowing final fatherly blessing on his favorite son. While Esau was out hunting deer for his father:

"Rebekah spoke to Jacob her son, saying, 'Indeed I heard your father speak to Esau your brother, saying, "Bring me game and make savory food for me, that I may eat it and bless you in the presence of the LORD before my death." Now therefore, my son, obey my voice according to what I command you. Go now to the flock and bring me from there two choice kids of the goats, and I will make savory food from them for your father, such as he loves. Then you shall take it to your father, that he may eat it, and that he may bless you before his death'" (27:6–10).

Rebekah's desperation to secure patriarchal blessing for Jacob bred deception and trickery. She believed her skills could make goat's meat taste and smell like choice venison (vv. 8–10) and make Jacob seem like Esau (vv. 15–17). To his credit, Jacob at first objected to Rebekah's plan (v. 12). The differences between him and Esau would surely not fool his father and might result in blessing being replaced with a curse as an apt punishment for deception. *"But his mother said to him, 'Let your curse be on me, my son; only obey my voice'"* (v. 13).

So with his mother accepting full responsibility for the scheme and bearing the curse should it occur, Jacob acquiesced and followed Rebekah's instructions.

Although Jacob received Isaac's blessing that day, the deceit caused severe consequences:

1. He never saw his mother after that.
2. Esau wanted him dead.
3. Laban, his uncle, deceived him.
4. His own family life was full of conflict.
5. He was exiled for years from his family. By the promise of God he would have received the birthright (25:23) even though his father intended otherwise. He didn't need to scheme this deception with his mother.

Rebekah had one final act of service for her favored son, but even that was tainted with deception. Fearing for his life, she instructed Jacob to *"flee to my brother Laban in Haran. And stay with him a few days, until your brother's fury turns away"* (27:43–44). Then, instead of telling Isaac the true reason for sending Jacob away, she convinced

Isaac that Jacob needed to find a wife from among their own relatives instead of marrying Canaanite women like Esau had.

The excuse was true, but it was not the full truth of the situation. Perhaps Isaac suspected Rebekah's real motives—they had, after all, been married for ninety-seven years at this point, so he knew her quite well—but he responded as Rebekah had hoped, by giving Jacob an intentional blessing and sending him to safety.

Honor your father
and your mother,
as the LORD your God
has commanded you.
—Deuteronomy 5:16

Then Isaac called Jacob and blessed him, and charged him, and said to him: 'You shall not take a wife from the daughters of Canaan. Arise, go to Padan Aram, to the house of Bethuel your mother's father; and take yourself a wife from there of the daughters of Laban your mother's brother.

"May God Almighty bless you,
And make you fruitful and multiply you,
That you may be an assembly of peoples;
And give you the blessing of Abraham,
To you and your descendants with you,
That you may inherit the land
In which you are a stranger,
Which God gave to Abraham".

So Isaac sent Jacob away, and he went to Padan Aram, to Laban the son of Bethuel the Syrian, the brother of Rebekah, the mother of Jacob and Esau.

—GENESIS 28:1–5

Although Rebekah never saw her son again, she believed God would fulfill His promise to make Jacob even greater than his brother. And He did . . . far beyond Rebekah's imagination. Through Jacob, later renamed Israel, came the twelve tribes, and from one of those tribes came the King of kings and Lord of lords. And by faith, Christians today are among the innumerable descendants of this extraordinary mother.

A Blessing for You

Like Rebekah, may you believe unwaveringly
in God's promises for your children.
Unlike Rebekah, may you understand that
you don't have to make these promises come true.
What God has promised, He will fulfill.

Rachel & Leah

MOTHERS OF A MIGHTY FAMILY

Genesis 29–35

*R*achel met her future husband while she was at work. She was a shepherdess and had come to water the flock when a stranger helped her uncover the well, kissed her in formal greeting, and told her that he was her cousin, Jacob, the son of her aunt Rebekah who had gone to marry Isaac ninety-seven years earlier. Rachel's reaction was entirely natural: *"She ran and told her father"* (Genesis 29:12).

From their first encounter, remarkably similar to how the servant of Abraham met Rebekah (24:15–22), it was evident that Jacob and Rachel were meant for each other; and a month after Laban, Rachel's father, welcomed Jacob to their home, Jacob requested her hand in marriage.

"Jacob loved Rachel; so he said, 'I will serve you [Laban] seven years for Rachel your younger daughter.' And Laban said, 'It is better that I give her to you than that I should give her to another man. Stay with me.' So Jacob served seven years for Rachel, and they seemed only a few days to him because of the love he had for her" (29:18–20).

Love and working to provide his service as a dowry combined to make Jacob happily remain during the first seven years in Laban's household, almost as an adopted son rather than a mere employee. But Jacob, the deceiver (27:1–29), was about to be deceived (29:22–25). Local marriage customs (v. 26), love for Rachel, and Laban's greed for more dowry (vv. 27–30) all conspired to give Jacob not only seven more years of labor under Laban but two wives—Rachel and her older sister, Leah—who were to become caught up in jealous childbearing competition (30:1–21). Such consanguinity was not God's will (2:24), and the Mosaic code later forbade it (Leviticus 18:18). Polygamy always brought grief, as in the life of Jacob.

"When the LORD saw that Leah was unloved, He opened her womb; but Rachel was barren" (Genesis 29:31).

The problem of infertility arose for the third time in Abraham's line. Like Sarah and Rebekah, Rachel, the beloved wife, could not conceive a child. Also like Sarah, Rachel soon faced the misery of knowing another woman would give her husband the family she could not. The difference was that Leah was of equal rank with Rachel, whereas Hagar was merely Sarah's servant. Still, Rachel must have been comforted by Jacob's love even as she watched her sister give him children. There was quite a cultural contrast when the one dearly beloved (vv. 18, 20, 30) had no children, whereas the one rejected did. Jacob might have demoted the unwanted Leah, but God took action on her behalf by giving her children. Leah also prayed about her husband's rejection (v. 33) and had been troubled by it, as seen in the names given to her first four sons (vv. 32–35). Leah saw each child as a chance to win Jacob's favor. But just as happens with so many struggling couples today who hope having a baby will improve their marriage, Leah's sons were not enough to secure Jacob's heart. He continued to favor Rachel.

Now when Rachel saw that she bore Jacob no children, Rachel envied her sister, and said to Jacob, "Give me children, or else I die!"
And Jacob's anger was aroused against Rachel, and he said, "Am I in the place of God, who has withheld from you the fruit of the womb?"
–Genesis 30:1–2

News between Abraham's nomadic progeny and their more-settled cousins might have been rare, but we can be almost certain that Rachel had heard of Sarah's desperate, ill-fated attempt to have children by Hagar. Nevertheless, as a desperate woman herself, Rachel undertook the same surrogacy scheme by giving her maid, Bilhah, to Jacob. After Bilhah bore two sons, Leah followed suit and gave Jacob her maid, Zilpah, who also gave birth to two sons while Leah had two more sons herself. Both sisters had been praying for children (29:33, 30:6, 17, 22), and both clearly knew the Lord is the One who sovereignly opens wombs (29:33, 35; 30:6, 18, 20, 23–24). But at this point the score was the still-unloved Leah six, plus two by proxy; the beloved Rachel zero, plus two by proxy.

Then finally all of Rachel's desperate waiting and pleading climaxed at the end of seven years with God's response.

God remembered Rachel, and God listened to her and opened her womb. And she conceived and bore a son, and said, "God has taken away my reproach." So she called his name Joseph, and said "The LORD shall add to me another son."

—GENESIS 30:22–24

Rachel properly ascribed her delivery from barrenness to the Lord, whom she also trusted for another son (vv. 23–24). Joseph's name means "he will add" or "may he add," and Rachel's choice of this name indicates both her thanks and her faith that God would give her another son. The birth of Joseph also appears to have calmed some the animosity between the sisters, as Scripture never records another disagreement between them, although their rivalry did continue among their sons.

Jacob was now ninety years old, and fourteen years of absence had not dulled Jacob's acute awareness of belonging to the land God had given to him. Because Mesopotamia was not his home and his contract with Laban was complete, he desired to return to "*my own place*" and "*my country*" (v. 25) with his growing family. Jacob's wish to return to Canaan was not hidden from his father–in–law, Laban, who wanted Jacob to stay and asked what it would take for him to do so. Jacob offered Laban a plan that could bless him while costing Laban almost nothing. Laban saw Jacob's plan as a small and favorable concession on his part to keep

Jacob's skills for further enlarging his herds and flocks. But Jacob was knowledgeable about sheep, goats, and cattle, and over the next six years his system ended up working more to his own advantage than that of Laban (v. 42) who had for years taken advantage of him. *"And Jacob saw the countenance of Laban, and indeed it was not favorable toward him as before. Then the LORD said to Jacob, 'Return to the land of your fathers and to your family, and I will be with you'"* (31:2–3). When Jacob first sought to leave at the end of his fourteen-year contract (30:25), God's timing was not right. Now it was, so God directed Jacob's departure, and in confirmation assured him of His presence. Finally, it was time to go home (31:38–41).

Like their aunt Rebekah, Rachel and Leah left the home of their youth forever in order to be with their husband in the Promised Land. There Jacob received a new name and divine affirmation of God's covenant with Abraham to make him *"a nation and a company of nations"* (35:9–12). This reminder of God's promised legacy came right before something terrible happened: Rachel died in childbirth (vv. 17–20). The dying mother named her newly born son Ben-Oni, which means "Son of my sorrow," but the grieving father renamed him Benjamin, "Son of my right hand," thus assigning his twelfth son a place of honor in the home. Although we do not know exactly when after this that Leah died, we do know that honor was finally accorded to Leah in death and in Jacob's request to be buried alongside his wife, as were his fathers (49:31). Burial alongside Rachel, the beloved wife, was not requested.

Rachel and Leah faced several extraordinary challenges, including sibling rivalry, a husband who preferred another wife, external pressure to bear many children, internal anguish at barrenness, other women in their husband's bedroom, discord between their father's family and their husband, dread of their brother-in-law's wrath, and—like Sarah and Rebekah—the expectation that they would be instruments used for God's purpose in establishing a powerful family legacy. Many of the challenges mothers face today usually are much different, but godly women still carry the responsibility to establish a legacy of faith in their children. The passage of millennia and vast changes in culture have not diminished this calling on the spiritual descendants of Sarah, Rebekah, Rachel, and Leah.

A Blessing for You

May the Lord make you *"like Rachel and Leah, the two who built the house of Israel; and may you prosper"* in your community (Ruth 4:11). May you establish a strong, godly legacy in your family.

Jochebed

She Entrusted Her Child to God

Exodus 1–2

In the centuries after the death of Joseph (circa 1804 B.C.), the last recorded event in Genesis, Israel's status in Egypt had changed radically from favor to enslavement (circa 1525–1445 B.C.). But despite the harsh conditions, the growth of the Israelite community was phenomenal! Their numbers grew from 70 men (Genesis 46:27) to 603,000 men, twenty years of age and older, thus allowing for a total population of about two million people (Numbers 1:46) who eventually departed from Egypt. The seed of Abraham was no longer an extended family, but a nation. God's promise that his descendants would be fruitful and multiply (Genesis 35:11–12) had indeed been fulfilled in Egypt.

Pharaoh instituted a number of measures to curtail their population, but his human power could not compete with God's continued blessing on Israel. Eventually, Pharaoh demanded that all his subjects become involved in murdering newborn Hebrew boys by drowning them in the Nile River (Exodus 1:22). One mother, Jochebed, managed to hide her beautiful baby for three months. *"But when she could no longer hide him, she took an ark of bulrushes for him, daubed it with asphalt and pitch, put the child in it, and laid it in the reeds by the river's bank. And his sister stood afar off, to know what would be done to him"* (2:3–4). She fully entrusted her child to God's safekeeping, and her careful actions to construct the ark of bulrushes, to set Moses afloat in the Nile (which technically complied with Pharaoh's order to cast infant boys into the river) but close to the royal bathing place, and to have his sister, Miriam, watch to see what would happen all indicate Jochebed's hope that something would work out right for the child.

And her hope was justified. God providentially used an Egyptian princess to override Pharaoh's death decree and protect the life of His chosen leader for the Israelites (vv. 5–10). Moreover, He gave Miriam the courage and presence of mind to approach the royal entourage and deftly convince the princess to pay the baby's own mother to nurse him.

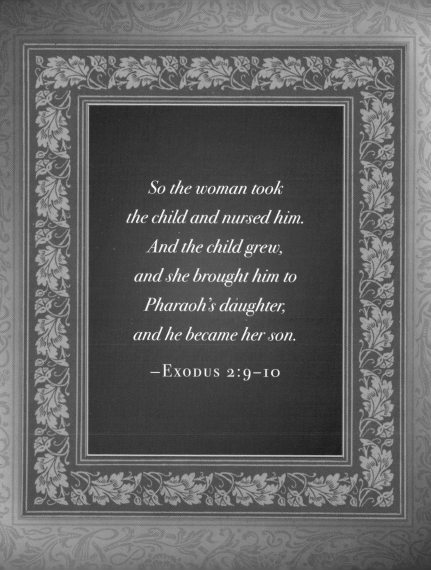

So the woman took
the child and nursed him.
And the child grew,
and she brought him to
Pharaoh's daughter,
and he became her son.

—Exodus 2:9–10

Moses needed a miracle to survive, and Jochebed was ready when the miracle came. Her faith in the Lord's provision was one of the first steps in Israel's march from Egypt. Did this faith come easily? Certainly not. Jochebed gave Moses everything she could, then gave him up—twice: once when she set him afloat in the river and once when she returned him to be raised by the princess. Both times Jochebed thought she'd never see her son again, but she entrusted her child to God's hands.

Later, as the adopted son of a princess, Moses undoubtedly was granted special privileges belonging to nobility, but none of these persuaded Moses to relinquish his native origin and faith, no doubt taught to him by Jochebed while she cared for him as a small boy. Rather, his spiritual maturity was such that when he came of age, he "*refused to be called the son of Pharaoh's daughter*" (Hebrews 11:24). As the son of Jochebed, Moses learned faith. As the son of a princess, he learned reading, writing, arithmetic, and perhaps one or more of the languages of Canaan. All these skills and experiences served him well when he became God's ambassador from Israel to Egypt.

A Blessing for You

At some point, every mother has to let her children go. May you do everything you can for your kids, then, like Jochebed, may you let them go and trust God to bless them far beyond your greatest hopes.

Deborah

A Light in a Dark Time

Judges 4–5

*I*n a time when *"the Israelites once again did evil in the eyes of the LORD"* (Judges 4:1 NIV) God let a neighboring king dominate them. After twenty years of suffering, they finally called out to God for help. And of course, God answered them, but His answer was different than usual—He sent a woman to lead them into forty years of peace.

We don't know much about Deborah's personal life other than the fact that she was *"the wife of Lappidoth"* (v. 4) and that she was *"a mother in Israel"* (5:7). What we do know is that she was a prophetess and that she *"was leading Israel at that time. She held court under the Palm of Deborah . . . and the Israelites came to her to have their disputes decided"* (4:4–5 NIV). Scripture also calls her a prophetess (v. 4), which refers to a woman who spoke God's Word as a teacher, not as a source of new revelation. The Old Testament mentions only three women who prophesied: Miriam (Exodus 15:20), Deborah, and Huldah (2 Kings 22:14; 2 Chronicles 34:22).

Deborah was an unusual woman of wisdom and influence who did the tasks of a judge, except for military leadership. Throughout Scripture we see that God can use women mightily for civil, religious, or other tasks—such as Huldah the prophetess (2 Kings 22:14), Philip's daughters in prophesying (Acts 21:8–9), and Phoebe a deaconess (Romans 16:1). Deborah's rise to the role of judge is an exception to God's plan for male leadership, but because the chosen general, Barak, failed to show the courage to lead courageously (Judges 4:8, 14), God rebuked his cowardice by declaring that a woman would slay Sisera (v. 9).

Deborah's judgeship came during a sad era in Israel. The book of Joshua records how the people were obedient to God while conquering the land, but then throughout the book of Judges, they were disobedient, idolatrous, and often defeated. A four-part sequence repeatedly occurred in this phase of Israel's history:

1. Israel's departure from God
2. God's chastisement in permitting military defeat and subjugation
3. Israel's prayer pleading for deliverance
4. God's calling of judges, either civil or sometimes local military champions who led in shaking off the oppressors. Fourteen judges arose, six of them military judges (Othniel, Ehud, Deborah, Gideon, Jephthah, and Samson).

In northern Israel where Deborah lived, the people had been suffering under Canaanite rule for twenty years. They had turned to other gods and surrendered their strength as warriors (5:8), but in her authority as judge, Deborah *"sent and called for Barak the son of Abinoam from Kedesh in Naphtali, and said to him, 'Has not the LORD God of Israel commanded, "Go and deploy troops at Mount Tabor; . . . against you I will deploy Sisera, the commander of Jabin's army, with his chariots and his multitude at the River Kishon; and I will deliver him into your hand"?'"* (4:6–7).

Deborah heeded God's will in calling upon a military leader to free His people, and even when that man's courage wavered, Deborah's remained strong.

"And Barak said to her, 'If you will go with me, then I will go; but if you will not go with me, I will not go!' So she said, 'I will surely go with you; nevertheless there will be no glory for you in the journey you are taking, for the LORD will sell Sisera into the hand of a woman.' Then Deborah arose and went with Barak to Kedesh" (vv. 8–9).

As Deborah foretold, Barak's troops decimated the Canaanite forces, and the mighty general Sisera was killed by a woman when he tried to hide in her tent (v. 21). This was truly unusual to have the greatest glory of the battle attributed to a woman, but as already mentioned, this was a time in Israel when women seemed to be stronger leaders than men. However, considering this leadership reversal, Deborah's song after the victory begins in a curious way . . .

*When leaders
lead in Israel, When
the people willingly
offer themselves,
Bless the LORD!*

–JUDGES 5:2

Deborah was the main leader in Israel, but she willingly offered the military glory to another, Barak, who should have been better suited for the role but who only accepted this leadership with great reluctance. This makes especially poignant Deborah's admonition to *"bless the LORD"* when leaders and followers are appropriately on task. Deborah's song is filled with this contrast between what should be and what actually has come to pass.

A mother must prepare her children to deal with the world as it is, while also instructing them about how it should be. In her wisdom, faith, and courage, Deborah proved herself an extraordinary mother to Israel.

A Blessing for You

Like Deborah, may you discern what is right
in a world full of wrong, and may you lead your
children to follow God's chosen path.

Hear, O kings! Give ear, O princes!

I, even I, will sing to the LORD;

I will sing praise to the LORD God of Israel. . . .

Village life ceased, it ceased in Israel,

Until I, Deborah, arose,

Arose a mother in Israel. . . .

My heart is with the rulers of Israel

Who offered themselves willingly with the people.

Bless the LORD!

—Judges 5:3, 7, 9

The Mother of Samson

PRENATAL DEDICATION

Judges 13–14

It is said that every child is a miracle, and often in Scripture we see that is literally the case. So it was with the wife of Manoah. Like many of the Hebrew matriarchs, she was barren, but then finally God promised this unnamed woman a miraculous son with a powerful destiny.

"The Angel of the LORD appeared to the woman and said to her, 'Indeed now, you are barren and have borne no children, but you shall conceive and bear a son. Now therefore, please be careful not to drink wine or similar drink, and not to eat anything unclean. For behold, you shall conceive and bear a son. And no razor shall come upon his head, for the child shall be a Nazirite to God from the womb; and he shall begin to deliver Israel out of the hand of the Philistines'" (Judges 13:3–5).

By this pre-incarnate appearance of the Lord Himself, the woman was given strict prenatal instructions for guarding her son's physical and spiritual development. He was to be a "*Nazirite to God from the womb.*" The word for *Nazirite* transliterates a Hebrew term meaning "dedication by separation." The Nazirite separated himself to the Lord by separating himself from:

1. grape products (Numbers 6:3–4);
2. the cutting of one's hair (v. 5); and
3. contact with a dead body (vv. 6–7).

In the same way, other aspects of the Law of Moses placed similar restrictions on the high priest by forbidding him to drink wine while serving in the tabernacle (Leviticus 10:9) and forbidding him to touch dead bodies (21:11). Furthermore, both the high priest's crown (Exodus 29:6; 39:30; Leviticus 8:9) and the Nazirite's head (Numbers 6:9, 18) are referred to by the same Hebrew word, signifying that the Nazirite's hair was like the high priest's crown. Like the high priest, the Nazirite was holy to the Lord (Exodus 28:36; Numbers 6:8) all the days

(Numbers 6:4–6, 8) of his vow. Such outward actions indicated an inner dedication to God, and Manoah's wife was instructed to begin her child's dedication immediately.

As soon as Manoah heard the news, he *"prayed to the LORD, and said, 'O my Lord, please let the Man of God whom You sent come to us again and teach us what we shall do for the child who will be born'"* (Judges 13:8). Such prayers for guidance still echo from the hearts of millions of godly parents today, and God always answers (Job 22:27–28; Psalm 86:6–7; Matthew 7:7–8; Philippians 4:6–7; 1 Thessalonians 5:16–18; Hebrews 4:16). God's answer to Manoah was powerful and direct—He appeared a second time to Manoah's wife, who immediately ran to bring her husband to meet Him (Judges 13: 9–10). In that meeting, the Angel of the Lord confirmed everything told to Manoah's wife (vv. 13–14).

We don't know why the Angel appeared primarily to Manoah's wife and not to Manoah. Perhaps the mother, who had, in effect, been commanded to take a variation of the Nazirite vow on behalf of her child, would play a greater role in Samson's spiritual growth than the father. Perhaps Manoah, who repeatedly questioned the Lord (vv. 11–12, 17), needed the additional verification of God's will by his wife's independent testimony. We do see clearly, however, that the Lord valued Manoah's wife as a full partner in raising her son and that His appearances to the woman did not violate His own rules regarding the husband as the head of the family. In fact, He reiterated that headship both by specifically answering Manoah's prayer with a second appearance and by patiently remaining to answer Manoah's questions and accept his sacrificial offering (vv. 19–20).

"When the Angel of the LORD appeared no more to Manoah and his wife, then Manoah knew that He was the Angel of the LORD. And Manoah said to his wife, 'We shall surely die, because we have seen God!' But his wife said to him, 'If the LORD had desired to kill us, He would not have accepted a burnt offering and a grain offering from our hands, nor would He have shown us all these things, nor would He have told us such things as these at this time.' So the woman bore a son and called his name Samson; and the child grew, and the LORD blessed him. And the Spirit of the LORD began to move upon him" (vv. 21–24).

As Samson grew to manhood, he revealed a weakness for unsuitable Philistine women (14:1; 16:1). With two godly parents, we don't know why Samson would be vulnerable in this area, but we can recognize the pain his choices caused Manoah and his mother (14:3). Most of us today know excellent parents who have been grieved by their own children's poor relationship choices, and like many contemporary parents, Samson's mother and father tried to talk him out of the mistake, eventually accepted his decision, and then tried to make the best of it by staying close to Samson as he journeyed into danger (v. 5). Scripture only mentions Samson's mother twice more when in short succession it's revealed that Samson was withholding information from his parents (vv. 6, 9), another indication of Samson's withdrawal from relationship with the godly people who raised him.

Scripture gives us a ray of hope, though, that Samson's parents could not see: *"But his father and mother did not know that it was of the LORD—that He was seeking an occasion to move against the Philistines. For at that time the Philistines had dominion over Israel"* (v. 4). The Philistines were not among the seven nations of Canaan that Israel was specifically forbidden to marry (Deuteronomy 7:1). Nonetheless Samson's choice of wife was seriously weak. Despite Samson's sin, God in His sovereignty was able to turn the situation to please Himself (Judges 14:4). The Lord used the opportunity to work against the wicked Philistines and provide gracious help to His people, not by raising an army but by unleashing the miraculous power of one man. Flawed though Samson was, this beloved son of Manoah and his wife was also a beloved child of God whose service to the Lord ultimately earned him a mention in the Hall of Faith passage in Hebrews (11:32). Samson did not earn this praise for his personal status or abilities, but instead he was recognized for what he had accomplished by faith in God in freeing God's people from a powerful enemy (Judges 16:28–31).

A Blessing for You

Like Samson's mother, may you dedicate your
children to the Lord from the womb and walk
alongside them in faith. May you never give up
on them, even when they make poor choices.
May you be assured that even when you cannot
walk alongside them anymore, the Lord
will be there creating paths of hope.

Abigail

MOTHER TO HER COMMUNITY

1 Samuel 25

*A*bigail *"was a woman of good understanding and beautiful appearance"* who was married to a rich man named Nabal who was *"harsh and evil in his doings"* (1 Samuel 25:3). Nabal's name literally meant "fool," which offers a profound insight into his character. "Fool" has the connotation of one who is "morally deficient."

While hiding out in the wilderness, David and his men had protected Nabal's flocks (vv. 7, 15–16), and upon hearing that Nabal was shearing his sheep, David sent ten men to collect their rightful compensation for the good they had done (v. 8). Nabal, however, refused to acknowledge his debt to David, asking, *"Who is David, and who is the son of Jesse? There are many servants nowadays who break away each one from his master. Shall I then take my bread and my water and my meat that I have killed for my shearers, and give it to men when I do not know where they are from?"* (vv. 10–11). This pretended ignorance of David was surely a sham. The knowledge of the young king-elect was widespread. Nabal pretended not to know to excuse his unwillingness to do what was right.

But one of Nabal's servants warned Abigail of what her husband had done, even adding, *"Consider what you will do, for harm is determined against our master and against all his household. For he is such a scoundrel that one cannot speak to him"* (v. 17). This strong testimony of one of Nabal's men affirmed both the value of David's protection and the poverty of Nabal's character.

Abigail's response was decisive. Because this happened on a feast day celebrating the shearing (v. 8), she immediately—and without telling Nabal—packed up the already-prepared food, then raced to meet David's army and prevent the slaughter of her household. Many of the sayings in Proverbs reflect the wisdom of bringing gifts to appease someone (17:8; 18:16; 19:6), particularly,

"A gift in secret pacifies anger, and a bribe behind the back, strong wrath" (21:14). Abigail knew that Nabal would disagree with her actions, but knowing the Lord's favor upon David (1 Samuel 25:28), she recognized the consequences involved in Nabal's cursing of David. By her actions, she chose to obey God rather than man (Acts 5:29), as a wife sometimes might need to do.

> *"Now when Abigail saw David, she dismounted quickly from the donkey, fell on her face before David, and bowed down to the ground. So she fell at his feet and said: 'On me, my lord, on me let this iniquity be! And please let your maidservant speak in your ears, and hear the words of your maidservant. Please, let not my lord regard this scoundrel Nabal. For as his name is, so is he: Nabal is his name, and folly is with him! But I, your maidservant, did not see the young men of my lord whom you sent. Now therefore, my lord, as the LORD lives and as your soul lives, since the LORD has held you back from coming to bloodshed and from avenging yourself with your own hand, now then, let your enemies and those who seek harm for my lord be as Nabal. And now this present which your maidservant has*

brought to my lord, let it be given to the young men who follow my lord. Please forgive the trespass of your maidservant. For the LORD will certainly make for my lord an enduring house, because my lord fights the battles of the LORD, and evil is not found in you throughout your days. Yet a man has risen to pursue you and seek your life, but the life of my lord shall be bound in the bundle of the living with the LORD your God; and the lives of your enemies He shall sling out, as from the pocket of a sling. And it shall come to pass, when the LORD has done for my lord according to all the good that He has spoken concerning you, and has appointed you ruler over Israel, that this will be no grief to you, nor offense of heart to my lord, either that you have shed blood without cause, or that my lord has avenged himself. But when the LORD has dealt well with my lord, then remember your maidservant'" (1 Samuel 25:23–31).

Abigail's plea to David was both wise and humble. She begged David for mercy, offered him a way to avoid bloodshed, gave him generous gifts of food, and affirmed her belief that God held David in special favor. Her perceptive insights into David's *"enduring house"* fit an essential feature of the Davidic Covenant (2 Samuel 7:11–16), and the fact that David *"fights the battles of the LORD"* shows her understanding that unlike the king previously desired by the people (1 Samuel 8:20), David was truly God's king. She knew God cared for His own as a man would his valuable treasure, and that David enjoyed the protection of divine providence, which destined him for great things. Abigail was certain that David would exercise effective rule over Israel after Saul's death, and she cautioned David that in the meantime he should not do anything to jeopardize his future, endanger his throne, or violate God's will by seeking personal vengeance in anger (25:23–31).

"Then David said to Abigail: 'Blessed is the LORD God of Israel, who sent you this day to meet me! And blessed is your advice and blessed are you, because you have kept me this day from coming to bloodshed and from avenging myself with my own hand. . . .

Go up in peace to your house. See, I have heeded your voice and respected your person" (25:32–33, 35).

Abigail saved her household, and then she faithfully went home to find her husband intoxicated and clueless of the near disaster. When Nabal sobered up, Abigail told him what had happened, and Nabal apparently suffered a paralyzing stroke before dying ten days later (25:37–38). Nabal was the product of his own wickedness, and his unwillingness to seek the counsel of others (25:17) ultimately led to his demise.

As soon as David heard that Abigail was a widow, he sent messengers to propose marriage for him, and again her response is immediate and gracious. *"She arose, bowed her face to the earth, and said, 'Here is your maidservant, a servant to wash the feet of the servants of my lord.' So Abigail rose in haste and rode on a donkey, attended by five of her maidens; and she followed the messengers of David, and became his wife"* (25:41–42). Her humble willingness to *"wash the feet of the servants of my lord"* is a beautiful precursor to the women who washed Jesus' feet (Luke 7:38; John 12:3) and to the Lord's own example in serving His disciples (John 13:4–5).

Although we only know of Abigail physically being the mother of one child—David's second-born son, Chileab, who apparently died young because he is never mentioned as a contender for the throne (1 Samuel 25:3)—Scripture clearly shows Abigail as a diligent mother to her household. Even though Nabal failed to lead as a father, Abigail was faithful to her commitments to her husband, household, and king, and she acted decisively, graciously, and wisely.

A Blessing for You

Like Abigail, may you serve the Lord and the people who rely on you faithfully, wisely, and humbly, regardless of your household circumstances.

The Mother of King Lemuel

SHE SHINES THROUGH HER SON

Proverbs 31

The Proverbs 31 description of the virtuous woman is one of the best-known passages in Scripture. What is often overlooked, however, is the origin of the passage. It was written by a king who said he learned this wisdom from his mother.

This final chapter of Proverbs contains two poems—the Wise King (31:2–9) and the Excellent Wife (31:10–31)—both of which are attributed to King Lemuel, whom ancient Jewish tradition identified as King Solomon, but who is otherwise unknown. If Lemuel is, in fact, Solomon, that means the mother who taught her son these wise sayings about excellent character was Bathsheba—a woman known more for scandal than virtue. Perhaps Bathsheba taught Solomon about his ancestor Ruth (Matthew 1:5–6), who had a spotless reputation, and then Solomon could have penned Proverbs 31:10–31 with Ruth in mind. After all, the passage parallels Ruth's life in many ways.

Regardless, Scripture does specifically record many instances of Solomon's great respect for mothers and for motherhood. For instance, one of the greatest examples of Solomon's wisdom was based on knowing that a mother would never harm her child and would only act in his best interests (1 Kings 3:16–28). Throughout the book of Proverbs Solomon frequently advises children to learn from both their parents (1:8; 10:1; 15:20), and he even personifies wisdom itself as a woman (1:20; 3:13–18; 4:5–9; 8:1–9:12). Furthermore, Solomon always respected Bathsheba, even bowing in her presence (1 Kings 2:19). Whatever Bathsheba's faults—whether or not she was, in fact, the mother of King Lemuel—she clearly helped her son Solomon become a wise man and great leader.

A Blessing for You

Whatever mistakes you've made in your own life,
may you still seek to instill God's wisdom
in your children, and may your relationship
with them remain strong.

Mary the Mother of Jesus

A Servant of God's Saving Grace

Matthew 1–2; Luke 1–2

*O*f all the extraordinary mothers in Scripture, one stands out above all others as the most blessed, most highly favored by God, and most universally admired by women. Indeed, no woman is more truly remarkable than Mary. She was the one sovereignly chosen by God—from among all the women who have ever been born—to be the singular instrument through which He would at last bring the Messiah into the world.

Mary herself testified that all generations would regard her as profoundly blessed by God (Luke 1:48). This was not because she believed herself to be any kind of saintly superhuman, but because she was given such remarkable grace and privilege. Her Son, not Mary herself, is the fountain of grace (Psalm 72:17).

Mary was a humble soul who maintained a consistently low profile in the gospel accounts of Jesus' life. Scripture reveals her as an average teenage girl betrothed to a working-class fiancé. If you had met Mary before her firstborn Son was miraculously conceived, you might not have noticed her at all. From everything we know of her background and social standing, not much about her life or her experience so far would be deemed very extraordinary.

When we first meet Mary in Luke's Gospel, it is when an archangel appeared to her suddenly and without fanfare to disclose to her God's wonderful plan. Scripture says, simply, *"The angel Gabriel was sent by God to a city of Galilee named Nazareth, to a virgin betrothed to a man whose name was Joseph, of the house of David. The virgin's name was Mary"* (Luke 1:26–27).

At the time of the Annunciation, Mary was probably still a teenager. It was customary for girls in that culture to be betrothed while they were still as young as thirteen years of age. Marriages were ordinarily arranged by the bridegroom or his parents through the girl's father. Mary was betrothed to Joseph, about whom we know next to nothing except that he was a carpenter (Mark 6:3) and a righteous man (Matthew 1:19).

Numerous godly women in Mary's ancestry, going all the way back to Eve, had fostered the hope of being the one through whom the Redeemer would come. But the privilege came at a high cost to Mary personally, because it carried the stigma of an unwed pregnancy. Although she had remained chaste, the world was bound to think otherwise. Even Joseph assumed the worst. We can only imagine how his heart sank when he learned that Mary was pregnant and knew he was not the father. Scripture says he was not willing to make a public example of her, but he was so shaken by the news of her pregnancy that at first he saw no option but divorce. Then an angel appeared to him in a dream and reassured him: *"Joseph, son of David, do not be afraid to take to you Mary your wife, for that which is conceived in her is of the Holy Spirit. And she will bring forth a Son, and you shall call His name JESUS, for He will save His people from their sins"* (Matthew 1:20–21).

Mary's amazement at learning that she would be the mother of the Redeemer must have been tempered significantly at the horror of the scandal that awaited her. Still, knowing the cost and weighing it against the immense privilege of becoming the mother of the Christ, Mary surrendered herself unconditionally, saying simply, *"Behold the maidservant of the Lord! Let it be to me according to your word"* (Luke 1:38).

Mary, filled with joy and bubbling-over praise, hurried to the hill country to visit her beloved relative Elizabeth. The angel had explicitly informed Mary about Elizabeth's pregnancy and it was natural for her to seek out a close relative who was both a strong believer and also expecting a child of her own, in order to share her heart and spend time rejoicing together in the Lord's goodness to both of them.

Elizabeth's immediate, prophetic response to the sound of Mary's voice gave Mary independent confirmation of all that the angel had told her. Mary replied with prophetic words of her own. Her saying is known as the *Magnificat* (Latin for the first word of Mary's outpouring of praise). It is really a hymn about the incarnation. Without question, it is a song of unspeakable joy, and the most magnificent psalm of worship in the New Testament. It is the equal of any Old Testament psalm, and it bears a strong resemblance to Hannah's famous hymn of praise for the birth of Samuel. It is filled with messianic hope, scriptural language, and references to the covenant of Abraham:

> *My soul magnifies the Lord,*
> *And my spirit has rejoiced in God my Savior.*
> *For He has regarded the lowly state of His maidservant;*
> *For behold, henceforth all generations will call me blessed.*
> *For He who is mighty has done great things for me,*
> *And holy is His name.*
> *And His mercy is on those who fear Him*
> *From generation to generation.*
> *He has shown strength with His arm;*
> *He has scattered the proud in the imagination of their hearts.*
> *He has put down the mighty from their thrones,*
> *And exalted the lowly.*

He has filled the hungry with good things,
And the rich He has sent away empty.
He has helped His servant Israel,
In remembrance of His mercy,
As He spoke to our fathers,
To Abraham and to his seed forever

–Luke 1:46–55

Mary's worship was clearly from the heart, and she was plainly consumed by the wonder of God's grace to her.

Throughout the Gospel accounts of Christ's earthly ministry, Mary appeared in only three scenes. The first of these occasions was during the wedding at Cana, when Jesus performed His first miracle. Mary was one of the first to see that the wine supply was not going to be enough, and, knowing that Christ had the means to solve this embarrassing social dilemma, she asked Him to do something about it. Scripture suggests His reply to Mary was a mild rebuke: *"Jesus said to her, 'Woman, what does your concern have to do with Me? My hour has not yet come'"*

(John 2:4). He was not being rude, and nothing suggests that Mary was in any way grieved or offended by His reply. His intent was not to wound, but to correct and instruct. Mary may have recalled a similar incident from Jesus' childhood when He was separated from His parents in Jerusalem. After a frantic search, they found Him at the temple, and Mary mildly scolded Him for allowing them to be worried. He replied, *"Why did you seek Me? Did you not know that I must be about My Father's business?"* (Luke 2:49). He was, in effect, disclaiming any notion that His earthly parents' interests could ever override the higher authority of His heavenly Father. At the Cana wedding, His message to Mary was similar. In spiritual matters, her earthly role as His mother did not give her any right to attempt to manage His mission as it pertained to fulfilling the Father's will on the Father's timetable. As a man, He was her Son. But as God, He was her Lord. Then He turned the water to wine.

After that, Mary remained in the background. She never again attempted to intercede with Him for miracles, special favors, or other blessings on behalf of her friends, her relatives, or anyone else.

Mary appeared again during Jesus' earthly ministry when the throngs who clamored for miracles from Christ had become larger than ever. Mark records that the demands of Jesus' ministry were such that He didn't even have time to eat (Mark 3:20). Jesus' own close family members began to be concerned for His safety. Scripture says they went to Him intending to physically pull Him away from the crowds and the heavy demands that they were making on Him (Mark 3:31–35). Once again, however, we see Mary learning to submit to Him as her Lord, rather than trying to control Him as His mother. She became one of His faithful disciples. She seems to have come to grips with the reality that He had work to do, and she could not direct it.

Mary ultimately followed her Son all the way to the cross, and on that dark afternoon when He died, she was standing nearby with a group of women, watching in grief and horror. The crucifixion was the third and final time Mary is recorded as appearing alongside Jesus during the years of His public ministry. Mary probably always had an inkling that this day would come. She had surely heard Jesus speak of His own death, and the cloud of this inevitable reality had probably hung over

Mary's mind since Jesus' infancy. It was no doubt one of the things she kept and pondered in her heart (Luke 2:19, 51). Luke's Gospel recounts how the first hint of impending tragedy crept into Mary's consciousness when Simeon prophesied about the infant Jesus: *"Behold, this Child is destined for the fall and rising of many in Israel, and for a sign which will be spoken against (yes, a sword will pierce through your own soul also), that the thoughts of many hearts may be revealed"* (vv. 34–35). Years later, as Mary stood watching a soldier thrust a sword into Jesus' side, she must have truly felt as if a sword had pierced her own soul also.

While Mary quietly watched her Son die, others were screaming wicked taunts and insults at Him. Her sense of the injustice being done to Him must have been profound. After all, no one understood Jesus' absolute, sinless perfection better than Mary did. She had nurtured Him as an infant and brought Him up through childhood. No one could have loved Him more than she did. All those facts merely compounded the acute grief any mother would feel at such a horrible sight. The pain of Mary's anguish is almost unimaginable.

Yet she stood, stoically, silently, when lesser men and women would have fled in fear or horror, shrieked and thrashed around in panic or despair, or simply collapsed in a heap from the overwhelming distress. Mary was clearly a woman of dignified grace and courage.

Mary seemed to understand that her steadfast presence at Jesus' side was the only kind of support she could give Him at this dreaded moment, but in the waning hour of Jesus' life, it was Jesus who came to her aid. Already in the final throes of death, He spotted Mary standing nearby with a small group of women and John, the beloved disciple. For the final time, Jesus acknowledged His human relationship with Mary. In his own Gospel account, John describes what happened: *"When Jesus therefore saw His mother, and the disciple whom He loved standing by, He said to His mother, 'Woman, behold your son!' Then He said to the disciple, 'Behold your mother!' And from that hour that disciple took her to his own home"* (John 19:26–27).

One of Jesus' last earthly acts before yielding up His life to God was making sure that for the rest of her life, Mary would be cared for.

That act epitomizes Mary's relationship with her firstborn Son. She was His earthly mother; but He was her eternal Lord. She understood and embraced that relationship. She bowed to His authority in heavenly matters just as in His childhood and youth He had always been subject to her parental authority in earthly matters (Luke 2:51). As a mother, she had once provided all His needs, but in the ultimate and eternal sense, He was her Savior and Provider.

Mary was like no other mother. Godly mothers are typically absorbed in the task of training their children for heaven. Mary's Son was the Lord and Creator of heaven. Over time, she came to perceive the full import of that truth until it filled her heart. She became a disciple and a worshiper, and her maternal relationship with Him faded into the background. That moment on the cross—Jesus placing His mother into the earthly care of John—formally marked the end of that earthly aspect of Mary's relationship with Jesus.

After Jesus' death, Mary appears only once more in the Bible. In Luke's chronicle of the early church, she is listed among the disciples who were praying together in Jerusalem immediately after the Ascension (Acts 1:14).

Mary devoted her life to her Son through His whole extraordinary journey on earth—from the angel's announcement of the Annunciation to worshiping with His disciples after His Ascension—and through it all Mary never claimed to be, or pretended to be, anything more than a humble handmaiden of the Lord. She was extraordinary because God used her in an extraordinary way. Her life and her testimony point us consistently to her Son. He was the object of her worship. He was the One she recognized as Lord. He was the One she trusted for everything.

A Blessing for You

Like Mary, may you devote yourself to your family from even before you learn you're pregnant. May you be there for them always. And may you entrust yourself—and your children—ever more faithfully to God throughout the journey of your life.

Mary the Mother of John Mark

A Brave Mother to the Faithful

Acts 12

Mary the Mother of John Mark

A Brave Mother to the Faithful

Acts 12

*A*n extraordinary mother quietly appears in the middle of one of the most dramatic stories about the fledgling church. You've probably read the passage many times without noticing her. The apostle Peter was heavily guarded while imprisoned in Jerusalem, but *"constant prayer was offered to God for him by the church. And when Herod was about to bring him out, that night Peter was sleeping, bound with two chains between two soldiers; and the guards before the door were keeping the prison. Now behold, an angel of the Lord stood by him, and a light shone in the prison; and he struck Peter on the side and raised him up, saying, 'Arise quickly!' And his chains fell off his hands"* (Acts 12:6–7), and the angel led him safely to a street just outside the prison. *"So, when [Peter] had considered this, he came to the house of Mary, the mother of*

John whose surname was Mark, where many were gathered together praying. . . . When they opened the door and saw him, they were astonished. But motioning to them with his hand to keep silent, he declared to them how the Lord had brought him out of the prison. And he said, 'Go, tell these things to James and to the brethren.' And he departed and went to another place" (vv. 12, 16–17).

This is the only time the Bible mentions Mary the mother of John Mark, but we can glean quite a bit of information about her:

1. She was probably a widow. The house is referred to as hers, not her husband's.

2. Because John Mark was the cousin of Barnabas (Colossians 4:10), we know that Mary was Barnabas's aunt.

3. She must have been a prominent supporter of the early church, because Peter knew he could go to her home to receive help and to reassure the church.

4. She must have been brave. The church was enduring persecution—James the brother of John had been martyred recently, and Peter seemed about to share that fate—but Mary still welcomed the church into her home, even at great personal risk.

We also learn about Mary's extraordinary nature through what we know of her son, who is called both John and Mark. A short time after Peter's escape, Barnabas and Paul visited Jerusalem and then took John Mark with them when they left again on a missionary journey (Acts 12:25). Six cities later, John Mark left the work and returned to Jerusalem (13:13). Whatever reason John Mark gave for leaving, Paul didn't accept it (15:38), and although his desertion did not hamper the mission, it did later create dissension between Paul and Barnabas (vv. 36–40), which was finally resolved (Colossians 4:10). In fact, while Paul was imprisoned in Rome, he specifically requested John Mark's help: *"Only Luke is with me. Get Mark and bring him with you, for he is useful to me for ministry"* (2 Timothy 4:11). Although he had once left Paul and Barnabas in shame, Mary's son recovered to persist as a devoted fellow worker, and he was used by God to write the Gospel of Mark.

So what does John Mark's story tell us about his mother, Mary?

1. Mary raised a believing son who loved the work of God enough to embark on a potentially dangerous missionary journey, and she unselfishly let him go.

2. Mary's son knew that when he was in trouble, he could go home to her.

3. Mary's son understood that failure isn't fatal and that he could return to serving the God of all grace. John Mark's restoration to useful ministry also was aided by his close relationship with Peter, who referred to him as *"Mark my son"* (1 Peter 5:13). Peter, of course, was no stranger to failure himself, and his influence on the younger man was no doubt instrumental in helping John Mark leave the instability of his youth and gain the strength and maturity he would need for the work to which God had called him. Other early accounts of the church indicate that John Mark wrote his Gospel based on the preaching of Peter.

This extraordinary son reflects the faith-filled influence of an extraordinary mother.

A Blessing for You

Like John Mark's mother, may you see your children grow to mature faith as you raise them among God's people and give them into His service.

Acknowledgements

Portions of *The Extraordinary Mother*
were adapted from the following books
written by John MacArthur and published
by Thomas Nelson, Inc. All copyrights
are held by the author.

The MacArthur Study Bible
The Macarthur Bible Study Series
12 Extraordinary Women

About the Author

JOHN MACARTHUR, one of today's foremost Bible teachers, is the author of numerous bestselling books that have touched millions of lives. He is pastor-teacher of Grace Community Church in Sun Valley, California, and president of The Master's College and Seminary. He is also president of Grace to You, the ministry that produces the internationally syndicated radio program "Grace to You" and a host of print, audio, and Internet resources—all featuring John's popular verse-by-verse teaching. He also authored the notes in The MacArthur Study Bible, which has been awarded the Gold Medallion and has sold more than 600,000 copies. John and his wife, Patricia, have four children (all married), who have given them thirteen grandchildren.

For more information about John MacArthur
and his Bible-teaching resources, contact Grace to You at:
800–55–GRACE (800–554–7223)
or www.gty.org